US WOMEN'S PROFESSIONAL SOCCER

BY JON MARTHALER

SUPER SOCCER

SportsZone
An Imprint of Abdo Publishing
abdobooks.com

Muskegon Area District Library
4845 Airline Rd, Unit 5
Muskegon, MI 49444-4563

abdobooks.com

Published by Abdo Publishing, a division of ABDO, PO Box 398166, Minneapolis, Minnesota 55439. Copyright © 2019 by Abdo Consulting Group, Inc. International copyrights reserved in all countries. No part of this book may be reproduced in any form without written permission from the publisher. SportsZone™ is a trademark and logo of Abdo Publishing.

Printed in the United States of America, North Mankato, Minnesota
092018
012019

THIS BOOK CONTAINS RECYCLED MATERIALS

Cover Photos: Andrew Bershaw/Icon Sportswire/AP Images, foreground; Shutterstock Images, ball
Interior Photos: Shutterstock Images, 1; Nuccio Dinuzzo/KRT/Newscom, 4–5; Vincent Laforet/Getty Images Sport/Getty Images, 6; John Biever/Icon Sportswire/AP Images, 8–9; Ronald Martinez/Getty Images Sport/Getty Images, 11; Jeff Gross/Getty Images Sport/Getty Images, 13; MacGregor/Topical Press/Hulton Archive/Getty Images, 15; Bob Donnan/Sports Illustrated/Getty Images, 17; Victor Decolongon/Getty Images Sport/Getty Images, 19; Andy Mead/YCJ/Icon Sportswire/Corbis/Getty Images, 21; Alan Schwartz/Cal Sports Media/AP Images, 23; Patrick Gorski/Icon Sportswire/AP Images, 25; Alex Menendez/AP Images, 27; Don Ryan/AP Images, 28

Editor: Bradley Cole
Series Designer: Laura Polzin

Library of Congress Control Number: 2018949111

Publisher's Cataloging-in-Publication Data

Names: Marthaler, Jon, author.
Title: US women's professional soccer / by Jon Marthaler.
Description: Minneapolis, Minnesota : Abdo Publishing, 2019 | Series: Super soccer | Includes online resources and index.
Identifiers: ISBN 9781532117466 (lib. bdg.) | ISBN 9781641856287 (pbk) | ISBN 9781532170324 (ebook)
Subjects: LCSH: North American Soccer League--Juvenile literature. | Soccer--United States--Juvenile literature. | Soccer for women--Juvenile literature. | Soccer players--Juvenile literature.
Classification: DDC 796.3346--dc23

TABLE OF CONTENTS

CHAPTER 1
THE SPARK: 1999 WOMEN'S WORLD CUP **4**

CHAPTER 2
WOMEN'S UNITED SOCCER ASSOCIATION **8**

CHAPTER 3
WOMEN'S PROFESSIONAL SOCCER HISTORY **14**

CHAPTER 4
WOMEN'S PROFESSIONAL SOCCER **18**

CHAPTER 5
NATIONAL WOMEN'S SOCCER LEAGUE **24**

GLOSSARY 30
MORE INFORMATION 31
ONLINE RESOURCES 31
INDEX 32
ABOUT THE AUTHOR 32

CHAPTER 1

THE SPARK: 1999 WOMEN'S WORLD CUP

The story of women's professional soccer in the United States starts with the 1999 Women's World Cup. If not for the Fédération Internationale de Football Association (FIFA) organizing that tournament, the United States might still be missing out on women's professional soccer.

The 1999 Women's World Cup Final was on the line as Brandi Chastain prepared for her penalty kick. This was just the third Women's World Cup ever. The United States had won the first tournament, held in China in 1991. Norway had won the second tournament in 1995 in Sweden.

In the eight years since the first tournament, women's soccer had become much more popular around the world. The people who organized the Women's World Cup took a big chance with

US keeper Brianna Scurry, *left*, teams up with Michelle Akers (10) and Brandi Chastain (6) to keep China scoreless.

Teammates hug Brandi Chastain as they celebrate their 1999 Women's World Cup victory.

the 1999 Cup and put the matches in the country's biggest stadiums. The crowds had been relatively small in Sweden four years earlier, but fans showed up in 1999. The stadiums were packed with screaming fans whenever the Americans played.

More than 90,000 people packed the Rose Bowl in Pasadena, California, to watch the final between the United States and China. It was the largest crowd ever to attend a women's sporting event. And 40 million more fans were watching on TV.

Neither team managed to score in regulation or overtime. The match went to a penalty shootout. American goalkeeper Brianna Scurry stopped a kick from China's Liu Ying. The save meant that if Chastain scored, the United States would win.

Chastain was not originally in the lineup to take penalty kicks. At the last moment, the coach moved her up the order to be the fifth shooter. He also asked her to take the kick with her left foot instead of her right to confuse the goalkeeper. With the stadium screaming, Chastain waited for the referee's whistle. When it blew, she ripped a kick with her left foot to the goalkeeper's left. The keeper dived at the ball, but she could not reach it as it scorched past her into in the corner of the net.

Chastain ripped off her jersey in celebration and fell to her knees. Her celebrating teammates mobbed her. Chastain's classic celebration ran on the cover of *Sports Illustrated*. It was voted the magazine's second-most famous cover of all time.

Chastain's kick launched women's professional soccer in the United States. Less than a year later, the first professional league in American history was announced.

CHAPTER 2

WOMEN'S UNITED SOCCER ASSOCIATION

The first Women's United Soccer Association (WUSA) game took place on April 14, 2001. It matched Chastain, playing for the Bay Area CyberRays, against superstar striker Mia Hamm, playing for the Washington Freedom. They were still teammates on the US women's national team (USWNT). But here they were rivals. In the second half, Hamm drove into the penalty area and got tangled up with Chastain. The referee blew her whistle for a penalty kick for Washington. Brazilian forward Pretinha scored the penalty, and the game ended 1–0 for Washington.

The 1999 Women's World Cup had convinced investors to buy into women's soccer. They put up $64 million and gave each team a salary cap of almost one million dollars. The best players in the world played in the WUSA, including every player

Mia Hamm's effortless control of the ball made her the star of the WUSA.

from the US team that won the 1999 Women's World Cup. Twenty-two games were broadcast on national TV.

The league's championship game was called the Founders Cup. The first Founders Cup in 2001 matched up the Atlanta Beat and the CyberRays. The teams finished with the same number of points in the standings. They were very evenly matched.

Chastain scored early in the match for Bay Area. Atlanta came back quickly, scoring twice for a 2–1 lead. But the CyberRays scored again before halftime. It was 2–2 after 45 minutes. With just seven minutes to go in the game, Chinese superstar Sun Wen scored for Atlanta to make it 3–2. Atlanta was close to the title. But Bay Area forward Tisha Venturini scored just moments later to tie the game at 3–3.

The game went to penalty kicks. Wen missed her kick for Atlanta. So did forward Charmaine Hooper. It left the game to Bay Area's Julie Murray. She made her kick, and the CyberRays won the championship.

Hamm was the biggest star of the new league. The league chairman called her WUSA's Michael Jordan. She scored 25 goals

Hamm and her USWNT teammates helped generate a lot of media attention for the WUSA.

over the three seasons of the WUSA. Other Americans such as Julie Foudy, Tiffeny Milbrett, and Chastain were also stars in the WUSA.

Hamm's team, the Washington Freedom, won one WUSA championship. It came in the 2003 Founders Cup championship game. Washington and Atlanta were tied 1–1 at the end of regulation. The game went to a sudden-death overtime. The next goal would win the game. Four minutes into overtime, an Atlanta defender fouled Washington forward Abby Wambach right outside the penalty area. It meant that the defender, Nancy Augustyniak, was sent off. Hamm stepped up to take the free kick after the foul, but the ball hit the crossbar and bounced away.

Just two minutes later, Washington's Jennifer Meier got the ball. She passed it behind the defense, and Wambach blasted the ball past the goalkeeper, giving Washington the championship.

The WUSA folded five days before the 2003 Women's World Cup. The league couldn't find enough businesses to advertise with the teams. TV ratings and attendance were also lower than they had hoped. Over the three seasons of the league, it lost nearly $100 million. Rather than continue to lose money, the league officials decided to stop playing.

Abby Wambach celebrates the goal that gave the Washington Freedom the Founders Cup Championship in 2003.

CHAPTER 3
WOMEN'S PROFESSIONAL SOCCER HISTORY

The WUSA was the first fully professional league in the United States, but it was far from the first league in the world. Women's leagues were established as far back as the 1930s in European countries such as Italy and France. Norway and Sweden followed.

Even earlier, the first famous women's soccer team was started at a factory in England during World War I. The Dick, Kerr and Company factory started a team to raise money for the war. The Dick, Kerr Ladies team grew in popularity. Thousands of people went to watch their games. They got so popular that the men's teams worried about competing with them. So in 1921, the Football Association (FA) called for leagues in England to ban women's soccer on their pitches. The ban was lifted in 1971.

A team member of the Dick, Kerr and Company factory team, *right*, takes on a member of the French Ladies International team during a game in 1925.

By the 1970s, women's soccer competitions were much more common. Sweden crowned its first national champion in 1973. By the 1990s, most European countries had formed top-tier leagues. The first official European championships were held in 1984. The first Women's World Cup was held in 1991.

Women's soccer was popular in the United States long before professional leagues were formed. Many US colleges started women's soccer teams in the 1970s. The first National Collegiate Athletic Association (NCAA) national championship was held in 1982. The University of North Carolina at Chapel Hill won that first NCAA title. As of 2017 North Carolina had the most championships with 21.

In the United States, the United Soccer Leagues W-League also played from 1995–2015. It was not a fully professional league, but it gave players somewhere to play after college. This was especially important in the years when no professional

WOMEN'S SOCCER BANNED

England wasn't the only place to ban women's soccer. France banned women's soccer until 1970. Brazil banned it until 1979.

The success of North Carolina and other powerful collegiate soccer teams in the United States helped promote women's professional and national team soccer.

league was playing. The Women's Premier Soccer League has also played as a semi-pro league since 1998.

There are women's soccer leagues all over the world today. The most popular are the leagues in Europe, as well as leagues in Australia and Japan. Many players from the United States play in leagues in other countries in the offseason.

CHAPTER 4

WOMEN'S PROFESSIONAL SOCCER

After the WUSA folded in 2003, supporters rallied to try to organize a new league. Rather than a regular season, WUSA played two exhibition tournaments in 2004 to try to keep fans interested in women's soccer. They featured only a few teams and borrowed stars from the remaining squads. By 2006 organizers were ready to announce a new league, but it took them until 2009 to start playing. When they finally launched, the new league had seven teams and was called Women's Professional Soccer (WPS).

Brazilian star Marta joined the new league in 2009. She had won the FIFA Women's Player of the Year award the previous three years. She would be the defining player of the WPS. In 2009 she played for the Los Angeles Sol. She led the league

The WPS was filled with international stars such as Brazil's Marta.

in scoring with 10 goals. The Sol won the regular-season championship but lost in the playoff finals to New Jersey's Sky Blue FC.

> **RECORD SETTER AND LOGO**
>
> Mia Hamm retired in 2004 as the leading scorer in US national team history. When WPS debuted, it used Hamm's silhouette as the basis for its logo.

The league soon ran into problems. The Sol folded after just one season. St. Louis folded partway through the next season. The league added several new expansion teams, but others folded just as quickly.

Marta moved to FC Gold Pride in Santa Clara, California, for the 2010 season. This time her team won the championship. FC Gold Pride ended the year with a 13-game unbeaten streak. Marta led the league with 19 goals and 24 points. She was named the league's Most Valuable Player (MVP) award.

FC Gold Pride went out of business at the end of 2010. Marta moved to the Western New York Flash and teamed up with Alex Morgan. Marta once again led the league in scoring

Marta was FC Gold Pride's MVP, helping her team defeat the Philadelphia Independence in the 2010 WPS championship game.

in 2011, with 10 more goals. And once again her team won the championship.

The 2011 championship match was one of the most exciting played in the WPS era. Western New York faced the Philadelphia Independence for the title. Canadian star Christine Sinclair scored in the 64th minute for Western New York. It looked like the Flash had secured the title, but Philadelphia came right back. With only three minutes to go in the game, Flash goalkeeper Ashlyn Harris blocked a shot but couldn't hang on. Independence forward Amy Rodriguez found the loose ball and scored on the far post to tie the game 1–1.

The match went into extra time. Western New York had a player sent off. Philadelphia couldn't capitalize on this advantage, and the game went to penalty kicks. Both teams made their first four kicks in the shootout. When Yael Averbuch, who had subbed in during extra time, buried the ball in the far right of the net, the Flash were perfect in penalty kicks. Then Harris stopped Philadelphia's fifth attempt, and Western New York was the champion.

Ashlyn Harris makes a diving save during the shootout to help the Flash win the championship.

At the end of 2011, the league got into a legal battle with one of its owners. The WPS ended up suspending operations because of the disagreement.

CHAPTER 5

NATIONAL WOMEN'S SOCCER LEAGUE

The National Women's Soccer League (NWSL) started in 2013. It was different from the leagues that came before it. Unlike WUSA and WPS, it wasn't run independently. The US Soccer Federation and the Canadian Soccer Association started the league and provided the salaries for the national-team players in the league. The teams themselves paid the rest of the players.

As had been the case in other leagues, the players from the USWNT were the stars of the league. For the first season, each NWSL team got three players from the American national team. USWNT star Lauren Holiday was the leading scorer and MVP in 2013. The top four NWSL scorers in 2013 were all US national team players.

When Julie Ertz isn't playing on the USWNT, she's commanding the midfield for the Chicago Red Stars.

Four teams remained from WPS: the Chicago Red Stars, Boston Breakers, Western New York Flash, and Sky Blue FC. In 2013 they joined the NWSL. New teams in Seattle, Portland, and Kansas City joined the league. In Portland the new team was owned by the same people who owned the Timbers in Major League Soccer.

The Portland Thorns won the first NWSL championship game in 2013. The team was on the road against Western New York. Tobin Heath scored in the first half, and it was 1–0 at halftime. With 34 minutes to go, Portland player Kathryn Williamson was sent off, leaving the Thorns with just 10 players for the rest of the game. Western New York couldn't score, though. Late in the game Christine Sinclair scored another goal, and Portland won 2–0.

The popularity of the American national team in the 2015 Women's World Cup helped make several NWSL players household names. Striker Alex Morgan and midfielders Carli Lloyd and Julie Ertz starred for both their NWSL teams and the national team.

With players such as Alex Morgan, the Portland Thorns have been one of the NWSL's top teams.

Samantha Kerr is the league's all-time leading scorer. The Australian scored 43 goals in the first five seasons of the NWSL. The league's best player might be defender Becky Sauerbrunn. She has played for Kansas City and Utah. Sauerbrunn was named the league's defensive player of the year in each of the first three seasons of the league. Through 2017 she also made the Best XI all-league team every year of the NWSL.

The Portland Thorns thank their fans for their support after a match in 2015.

The Portland Thorns have been the most popular team in the NWSL. They have led the league in attendance every year. Portland's average attendance is more than double the next-best team. The Thorns have also been good on the field. Portland has won two NWSL championships. In 2016 they also won the Supporters' Shield for having the league's best regular-season record.

The teams in Boston and Kansas City have folded. The Western New York Flash moved to North Carolina. Three other teams have joined the league and are trying to replicate Portland's success. The Houston Dash, Orlando Pride, and Utah Royals are all owned by MLS teams, like Portland. They share stadiums and staff with the MLS teams. This makes it easier for them to be successful. Orlando's first home game ever in 2016 set the league's attendance record at 23,403. Morgan scored in a 3–1 win against Houston.

Social media has made it much easier for the NWSL to succeed. WUSA and WPS had to depend on newspapers and TV stations to report news about the leagues. The NWSL uses Instagram, Facebook, and Twitter to get news to fans. The league also can stream all of its games on YouTube instead of trying to get TV stations to broadcast the games.

The history of women's pro soccer in the United States has been complicated. There have always been star players, but leagues have come and gone. The NWSL is the first professional league to last more than three seasons. Unlike the WPS and WUSA, it is thriving.

GLOSSARY

Best XI
The best players at each position are named to the Best XI team at the end of the season.

extra time
Two 15-minute periods added to a game if the score is tied at the end.

folded
Went out of business.

midfielder
A player who stays mostly in the middle third of the field and links the defenders with the forwards.

penalty area
The box in front of the goal where a player is granted a penalty kick if he or she is fouled.

penalty kick
A play in which a shooter faces a goalkeeper alone; it is used to decide tie games or as a result of the foul.

penalty shootout
A tiebreaking shootout after stoppage time to decide who wins a game.

pitch
The soccer field.

salary cap
A limit on the amount of money that teams can pay players.

sent off
When a player is removed from the field, either for two cautions or a serious foul, for the duration of the game.

striker
A player whose primary responsibility is to create scoring chances and make goals.

Women's World Cup
A global soccer tournament that takes place every four years in a different country.

30

MORE INFORMATION

BOOKS

Christopher, Matt. *Mia Hamm.* New York: Little, Brown and Company, 2015.

Kortemeier, Todd. *Make Me the Best Soccer Player.* Minneapolis, MN: Abdo Publishing, 2017.

Kortemeier, Todd. *Total Soccer.* Minneapolis, MN: Abdo Publishing, 2017.

ONLINE RESOURCES

To learn more about women's professional soccer, visit **abdobooklinks.com**. These links are routinely monitored and updated to provide the most current information available.

INDEX

Atlanta Beat, 10–12
Averbuch, Yael, 22
Bay Area CyberRays, 8, 10
Boston Breakers, 26, 29
Chastain, Brandi, 4, 7, 8, 10, 11
Chicago Red Stars, 26
Dick, Kerr Ladies, 14
Ertz, Julie, 26
FC Gold Pride, 20
FIFA, 4, 18
Football Association (FA), 14
Foudy, Julie, 11
Founders Cup, 10–11
Hamm, Mia, 8, 10–12, 20
Harris, Ashlyn, 22
Heath, Tobin, 26
Holiday, Lauren, 24
Hooper, Charmaine, 10
Houston Dash, 29

Kerr, Samantha, 27
Lloyd, Carli, 26
Los Angeles Sol, 18–20
Marta, 18–20
Meier, Jennifer, 12
Milbrett, Tiffeny, 11
Morgan, Alex, 20, 26, 29
Murray, Julie, 10
National Women's Soccer League (NWSL), 24–29
Norway, 4, 14
Orlando Pride, 29
Philadelphia Independence, 22
Portland Thorns, 26, 28–29
Pretinha, 8
Rodriguez, Amy, 22
Scurry, Brianna, 7
Sinclair, Christine, 22, 26
Sky Blue FC, 20, 26
Sweden, 4, 6, 14, 16

United Soccer Leagues W-League, 16–17
University of North Carolina, 16
Utah Royals, 27, 29
Venturini, Tisha, 10
Wambach, Abby, 12
Washington Freedom, 8, 11–12
Wen, Sun, 10
Western New York Flash, 20, 22, 26, 29
Women's Premier Soccer League, 17
Women's Professional Soccer (WPS), 18, 20, 22–23, 24, 26, 29
Women's United Soccer Association (WUSA), 8, 10–12, 14, 18, 24, 29
Women's World Cup, 4–7, 8, 10, 12, 16, 26
Ying, Liu, 7

ABOUT THE AUTHOR

Jon Marthaler has been a freelance sportswriter for more than 15 years. He writes a weekly soccer column for the *Star Tribune* in Minneapolis, Minnesota. Jon lives in St. Paul, Minnesota, with his wife and their daughter.